96 143

THE SILENCE OF THOMAS

BRUNO FORTE

THE SILENCE
OF THOMAS

Foreword by Aidan Nichols

New City

London

First published as *Il silenzio di Tommaso*
by Edizioni Piemme
Cassale Monferrato, Italy
© 1998 Edizioni Piemme

First published in English
by New City
Unit 17
Sovereign Park
Coronation Road
London NW10 7QP

Translated by David Glenday
English translation © New City 2003

Cover Design by
Tomeu Mayans

British Cataloguing-in-Publication Data
A catalogue record for this book is available from the British Library

ISBN 0 904287 85 8

Typeset by
New City, London

Printed and bound in Great Britain by
The Cromwell Press, Trowbidge, Wiltshire

Contents

Foreword

Something odd happened to Thomas Aquinas in Naples on (or about) 6 December 1273. What was it, and what were its implications not only for him but for Christians at large? This is the topic of Father Bruno Forte's poetic sequence *Il silenzio di Tommaso*, 'The Silence of Thomas'.

The occurrence – at once a spiritual experience of a very high order and a physical breakdown – took place during Thomas's celebration of Mass and it ended his career of teaching and writing. Actually, it was not so surprising that Thomas's life should draw to its close in such a way. He was a workaholic who had driven himself unrelentingly to study, lecture, dictate, all in the service of Catholic truth. His devotion, notably at Mass, his absorption in prayer, and the strong sense his theology conveys of the mystery of the God to whom we are united in Christ: these are well evidenced. We are more surprised perhaps that a modern professor of theology, albeit himself a priest and a Neapolitan, should write poetry on the topic. Any poetry, but above all, poetry that celebrates the collapse of theology into silence. To mitigate the shock, here are a few points we can bear in mind.

First, poetry is not alien to theology, not even to scholastic theology. Crucial to the Bible, it enlivens the Liturgy which is itself, after Scripture, the principal monument of Tradition. A number of the Fathers for example, Gregory Nazianzen, Ambrose, Ephraem used it, wrote it. The mediaeval divines knew its power to

7

advance understanding through the inroads a
disciplined imagination can make on the revealed
Infinite that is Christian truth. Thanks to the hymns
and sequence he wrote for the Office and Mass of
Corpus Christi, Thomas belongs with the practitioners
in this guild. As so often in Christian poetry, praise and
humility are the content of his verse, just as they are
the preconditions of its making. And what praise and
humility have in common is wonder, the root of the
mind's first stirrings when moved to explore the God of
love. A theologian who writes poetry is not, then, so odd
a creature after all.

Secondly, if the Mass was the moment of Thomas's
simultaneous breakthrough and breakdown, the occasion
when the Glory descended with results at once wonderful
and terrible to behold, then a modern theologian-poet
whose work unfolds from the Eucharistic mystery is well
placed to be the interpreter of Thomas's Passion. It is
from the Eucharistic centre that Forte's theology moves
out, into the embrace of the Trinity which is the Mass's
source. In his thought, God is the eternal play of: the
Silence, the Word, and the Encounter, the communion
which originates all being, embodied in the story of
Jesus, made our destiny too by the Spirit in the Church.
Not for nothing does Forte include *Il silenzo di
Tommaso* within that portion of his writings he terms a
'poetics of hope', for the Eucharistic rapture that signals Thomas's death tells us of the future-orientation of

the blessing this sacrament brings. In the Eucharist, in Thomas's own words, not only is 'the mind filled with grace' as 'the memory [or, better, the presence] of [Christ's] Passion is renewed'. More even than this, 'a pledge of future glory is given us'.

Thirdly and finally, Thomas is a thinker who, despite his reputation for abstraction, offers us a metaphysic of the concrete, and concrete is the stuff of poetry, not least of the poetry offered here. Abstraction has its place in Thomism, not to deflect attention from the concrete but, on the contrary, to help us identify the many formalities under which the concrete can be approached, the many aspects which make up its diamond. That things are (existence) and what they are (essence) are equally, for Aquinas, stimuli to admiration. Forte resembles another Christian thinker-poet, Charles Péguy, in the warmth of feeling he conveys for creation, for the earth and its fruits, and for family and friends, what the Italians call *i suoi cari*, a phrase whose intimacy the English 'one's loved ones' fails to convey.

And like Péguy, he gives the lie to the prophets of secular modernity when they claim, falsely, that such loves cannot survive attachment to a transcendent God, whose Face is hidden in the silence of his unutterable otherness. Forte's Thomas addresses the Lord in Péguy's style, with that freedom of spirit the New Testament terms 'boldness', *parrhesia*. For, as the texts given in this book insinuate, Love can use the failure of language, the rupture of relationships, the breakdown of the body, to usher us through the Paschal mystery into the light of Trinitarian day. Thomas did not, I believe, at the end of his life consider his theology 'straw' in the sense of rubbish – even compared with the vision of the divine Thou. (Words recorded at his death-bed make this fairly plain.) But he did come to see it as only a beginning. ('Straw' was a common term then for Scripture's literal sense.) When the Spirit and the Bride say 'Come!', there is so much more.

Aidan Nichols, O. P.

A Word from the Author

On the twenty-fifth anniversary of my ordination to the priesthood, I dedicate this book to all those for whom the Lord wanted me to be a priest. I thank Him for his countless gifts, aware of my failures to respond, which I consign to His mercy, and trusting unconditionally in His faithfulness for the future. To all I would want to say how great a gift the Priesthood is, a gift I love immensely; and how full and beautiful can be a life spent in that gift. I would want, too, to say that into the welcoming hands of the one who celebrates the Eucharist is entrusted – for the world – a foretaste of that Beauty, which transcends all knowing and which only the modesty of praise can least inadequately approach. This too, perhaps, was what Thomas perceived in that celebration of the Bread of life when his face was flooded with tears and his heart with silence...
Tibi soli Deo omnis honor et gloria!

Naples, April 18th 1973/1998

11

May this contemplative resting
at the last threshold
also be in special memory of –
and in blessing upon –
Gabriella Fusco
and Fr Rosario Maglia,
who loved these pages,
and Brother Max Thurian,
who was not able to read them:
the communion that bound us here
is kept safe now,
stronger than death itself,
in the welcoming silence of God...

Why did Thomas of Aquinas fall silent in the last months of his life? His biographers and interpreters have been fascinated by this enigma. From celebrating Mass on 6 December 1273, the 'Magister', who until the previous day had written or dictated his works to several secretaries at once, neither wrote nor dictated again until his death on 7 March 1274. He was, as it were, struck dumb, in a way that defies medical explanation, since he remained completely clear in his mind, was able to attend to his spiritual duties and to take decisions when called upon to do so.

What had happened to this man, this singular teacher of knowledge and loving witness to faith? The sources offer various clues, interpretations accumulate, but the mystery seems to remain...[1]

---

[1] Cf. *Fontes Vitae S. Thomae Aquinatis notis historicis et criticis illustrati*, ed. D. Prümmer and M.-H. Laurent, Toulouse, no date [originally 6 fascicules published in 'Revue Thomiste' from 1911 to 1937]. Particular reference will be made to William of Tocco, *Hystoria beati Thomae Aquinatis*, ed. Prümmer, in Fontes, 65-145, and to the *Processus canonizationis Neapoli*, ed. M.-H. Laurent, in *Fontes*, 265-407 (the Process took place from 21 July to 18 September, 1319). Among the interpretative reconstructions of Thomas's 'collapse' cf. J.A.Weisheipl, *Tommaso d'Aquino. Vita, pensiero, opere*, Milan 1994, pp. 324-334, and J.-P. Torrell, *Tommaso d'Aquino. L'uomo e il teologo*, Casale Monferrato 1994, pp. 324-330. Of particular interest is the unfinished research of R. Cacòpardo, *Se veramente Tommaso d'Aquino, come scrisse Dante, fu assassinato*, Milan, 1995.

*T*homas was often overtaken by a so-called abstractio mentis, but this became even more frequent in his last year. On Passion Sunday 1273, while celebrating Mass in the church of San Domenico Maggiore in Naples, he seemed to be overwhelmed by the divine mysteries: tears flooded from his eyes, and his mind seemed completely taken up elsewhere, so much so that he had to be shaken to make him continue.[2] This often happened that Lent, especially at Compline, when verse 9 of Psalm 70 (*7l*) was sung: 'Do not cast me off in the time of old age; do not forsake me when my strength is spent.'[3]

[2] Cf. William of Tocco, chap. 29, 103: the place is indicated with the expression 'in conventu Neapolitano,' referring to the Dominican house of San Domenico Maggiore in Naples.

[3] 'Visus fuit etiam frequenter, cum cantaretur ille versus in Completorio quadragesimali tempore: "Ne proicias nos in tempore senectutis, cum defecerit virtus mea", quasi raptus et in devotione absorptus multis perfundi lacrymis,' William of Tocco, idem.

In the midst of life
I weep for this earth
I love.
I weep
because these eyes of flesh
will see no more
the sun, the sky,
the sea, the hills,
the trees, the stars,
the day,
habitation of my thinking,
and the night,
guardian of my dreams.
I weep
because these eyes of mine
will look no more
upon beloved faces,
messengers of hope,
bridges thrown across
the void of loneliness.
I weep
because these hands
will no more touch
this matter
fragile yet sublime,
solid yet corruptible,
noble yet suspended
over the abyss of nothingness.

I weep
because these ears
will no more listen
to the music,
tragic yet sweet,
that fills life's silences.
I weep,
not for what will come –
I know what awaits me –
but for what is now,
which I must leave.
I weep for this life,
the life You gave me.
To love
this passing, fleeting earth,
to love it as I do
with faithful passion
is not to love You less,
you know.
Your crucified flesh
is leaven
transfiguring all things
with endless tenderness.
Yes, I weep for love
of all that passes,
of this brief moment,
home forever
of Your eternity.

And You,
do You not weep
with me
in Your eternal
Gethsemane?

Cast me not off, then,
when my tears
are done:
in that time
without tears,
hide me again,
I beg You,
in Your tears
of eternal love.

According to Reginald, Thomas's secretary and confessor, on 6 December 1273 ('a festo beati Nicolai circa'), while celebrating Mass in the chapel of St Nicholas in San Domenico Maggiore in Naples, Thomas experienced a deep transformation ('fuit mira mutatione commotus'). 'After that Mass he neither wrote nor dictated anything else, and he hung up his writing implements: he had reached the third part of the Summa, the treatise on Penance.'[4]

---

[4] 'Et post ipsam Missam numquam scripsit neque dictavit aliquid, immo suspendit organa scriptionis in tertia parte Summae, in tractatu de Poenitentia,' Processus, no. 79, 376 ff. This information is provided by Bartholomew of Capua, who passes on the testimony of John del Giudice, himself informed by Reginald.

Because of Your flesh
the dead will speak
words full of love.
Dumb silences will end,
the ancient fear of loving
will be no more.
And then
silence and word
will embrace.
The wounds of Your glorious Body
will speak words unsaid,
guardians
of time's infinite pain.
There will be joy
without end.
More,
there will be the Kingdom:
You the all-in-all,
and the whole world
risen
because of Your flesh,
crucified Love...

> *'On the willows there*
> *we hung up our harps...*
> *How could we sing the Lord's song*
> *in a foreign land?'*
> (Psalm 137, 2 and 4)

Harp on willow hung,
the thought of home
grows strong in silence.
Will words ever sing
this soul's open wound?
When the pain is exile,
home is nearer:
and quiet love
becomes the keeper
of what cannot be said,
the icon of farewell.

Reginald does not understand and insists that the Master begin dictating again, 'Father, why have you set aside a work so great, begun for the praise of God and the world's enlightenment?' Thomas replies, 'I cannot.' Reginald persists, and the Master confides, 'I cannot. Everything I have written now seems as so much straw in comparison with what I have seen and what has been revealed to me.'[5]

[5] 'Pater, quomodo dimisistis opus tam grande quod ad laudem Dei et illuminationem mundi coepisti?' Cui respondit dictus frater Thomas: 'Raynalde, non possum'...'non possum quia omnia quae scripsi videntur mihi paleae respectu eorum quae vidi et revelata sunt mihi,' *Processus*, no. 79, 376 ff.; cf. William of Tocco, chap. 4, 120.

Straw:
language,
inessential, flawed,
fragile flute
to call forth the abyss,
succession of words,
merest signpost
to the hidden spring
of speech.
Just as,
taken from the sun-blessed fields,
the full grain is ground
into flour that will feed,
bespeaking the taste
of the bread-to-be,
so too our talk,
burnt by the suns
of speech grown ripe,
turns into rapid signals,
promise of silences
to be savoured,
succession
of patience,
and of listening...

Listen:
from deep, deep silences
comes the word

in gentle enunciation
of falling cadences
pregnant with life.
Listen:
to the birth in silence
of the fruitful word,
home of the living.
In silence
listen
to the Word.
Listen...

Winnowing time
has come,
now the straw
is separated from the grain:
no more can words
draw pictures.
Defeat by silence
is victory:
our night's Adversary
is victorious
at the ford
of our eloquent
silence.

                  'Reginald, I cannot!'

Hitherto tireless, Thomas now needs rest. He is sent to the Castle of San Severino, north of Salerno, to his sister, the countess Theodora, who comes out to meet him. Thomas is hardly able to speak. Theodora turns to Reginald: 'What ails Brother Thomas? He is entirely out of himself and has barely said a word to me.' Reginald replies: 'The Master is often taken up in the spirit when he enters into deep contemplation, but I have never seen him away from his senses for as long as this.'[6] After some days, Thomas's sister – 'deeply distressed' – watches them leave, without there having been any significant change in her brother's condition.

[6] 'Frequenter Magister in spiritu rapitur, cum aliqua contemplatur, sed nunquam tanto tempore sicut nunc vidi ipsum sic a sensibus alienum,' William of Tocco, chap. 47, 120.

You love me:
why do You not
smell the fire's scent?
I cannot pass again
the threshold:
why does this seem to You
a silence without reason?
Words full of love
are what I long
to say to You!
But they too –
would they not be
mere straw,
good only to be burnt?
The fire
that flames in my heart,
wounded by love,
does it not give
invisible perfumes
that touch the soul?
Is not Your desolation too
love's touch?
Has not my silence
spoken to You
the deep secret
of the hidden
pearl?

They return to Naples at the end of December or the beginning of January. Around them there gathers the usual group of very varied brethren and friends.[7]

Later, during the canonization process, all will recall Thomas's preaching, and a few miraculous events, which seem almost to presage what is to come. For example, 'the very bright star that comes in through the window and rests for a while on Thomas's head...'

[7]In the process of canonization there appear, among others, the names of William of Tocco, James of Caiazzo, John of Boiano, Leonard of Gaeta, Peter of San Felice, all religious who unanimously underline the austerity and spiritual intensity of Thomas. Bartholomew of Capua, who as a young man had frequented the Dominican house in Naples, affirms that he saw Thomas on several occasions and provides information gathered from several witnesses, such as Reginald of Piperno, John Del Giudice, John of Caiazzo and John of San Giuliano. Ptolomy of Lucca had also lived in Naples with Brother Thomas, whose student and occasional confessor he was. Bonfiglio Coppa and Brother James of Salerno are called 'fratres', but also 'famuli' or 'servitores' of the Master: their devotion and attachment to Thomas showed themselves in the fact that often they hid themselves to be able to observe him at prayer. The 'socious continuus' of Thomas, however, was Reginald of Piperno (Privernum), the Master's faithful secretary and co-worker. Among the laymen mentioned in the Process are John Blasio, a judge, rather imaginative in his recollections; John Coppa, 'notarius'; John of Gaeta, 'zecca-denarius'; Peter Brancaccio, 'miles'.

The beloved faces return,
full of expectation,
lined with affection,
marked by memory.
Speaking compassion,
with arrows of sorrow
they return, and strike
at my soul's door.
Their hunger,
their questions, their joys –
will they rescue
the hostage
I have become
on the long-trod
roads of silence?
Where is the threshold?
Where does the love
that has pierced me
become flight
or last abandonment?
Given up to You,
my all,
I listen:
keep company
with Your heart that suffers –
that is what I must do,
and that is all I can.

THE STAR

Hidden in the skies of night
the star
appears, and disappears.
Flickering light,
across the gulf of distance,
for a sudden moment
it lets itself be near.
Its beam,
victor over ultimate separation,
parable of the Word,
lights up
the night's infinite silences:
still keeping safe
from indiscreet grasp
its luminous source,
ever at peace and ever alive.
In the night
the surpassing star
– the clear, sovereign star –
appears,
and disappears:
beyond the humble appearance
there rests the hidden star
in most substantial humility...

Soon after, Thomas, accompanied by his secretary Reginald and Brother James da Salerno, sets out once more in obedience to the Pope. Gregory X has called a Council at Lyons for 1 May 1274, in the hope of reaching an understanding with the Greeks, and Thomas, who in 1263 had written the Contra errores Graecorum *at the request of Urban IV, must be present, bringing a copy with him. When the travellers have passed Teano, an accident happens. Thomas knocks his head against the branch of a tree which has fallen across the road. Badly shaken ('fere stupefactus'), he insists on continuing the journey.*[8]

To distract him, Reginald makes conversation, suggesting that Thomas is sure to become a cardinal. Thomas, his mind entirely clear, replies: 'Reginald, you may rest assured that I will continue as I am.'[9]

[8] Processus, no. 78, 374-376.

[9] 'Raynalde, sis securus quod ego numquam in perpetuum mutabo statum,' ibid.

Why travel elsewhere
the ways of silence,
the soul's deep winding ways,
where the door opens
on to the last,
the greatest mystery?
Why is one place not enough,
an island,
a cell,
a prison of infinity,
where spirit may journey,
free, towards home?
Destiny?
The journey –
parable of life,
deep, wandering root
hidden from the plant,
voyage of the flesh,
that is,
heart's journey.
No fixed abode
for the pilgrim of the deep:
for him
all lands are home,
all homes
a foreign land.
And thus it is
that for the one

who seeks the Face
hidden in loneliness,
upon farewell
follows farewell.
Like an exodus without return
the great journey
leads
to life's threshold...

It is the hour!

It is the hour!
A beckoning,
a touch,
a hasty drawing back
from the long-trod paths
of silence,
from this journeying
in well-known lands,
by well-known seas and hills,
to give myself
to the great journey
towards the final shore,
unknown,
dark.
The frontier I had but felt
is suddenly there,
painfully, fleetingly
near:
in Your Gethsemane,
mine;
in Your desolation,
the last nakedness
of my heart
nailed
to earth's cross.

From Montecassino the Benedictines send Thomas a messenger inviting him to be their guest, and posing him a question concerning a passage from the writings of St Gregory about divine foreknowledge and human freedom. Thomas chooses to respond orally. His brief message to the monks will be copied by them into the margin of Gregory's work. With great clarity the Master shows how the difference between the divine and human planes means that there is no relation of necessity between the one and the other. The fact of seeing someone carrying out an act does not mean obliging him to do it. And yet, the ultimate Mystery remains greater than our hearts...

FREEDOM

A child is innocent,
and so is forgetting,
absence of future
or of past:
only the present
is responsible.
Watched by eternity,
the fleeting moment
tastes
the bitter sweet
fruit of freedom.
That love
which acted to create
is sovereign respect,
infinite humility.
Before the abyss
of the choosing heart
the Eternal
goes barefoot:
the creature's present
is holy ground.
Infinity
abbreviates itself
that the other
may rest free
in the welcoming womb
of Mystery.

> *'In finem nostrae cognitionis*
> *Deum tamquam ignotum cognoscimus'*
> *(Thomas of Aquinas*, In Boetium
> de Trinitate, *q.1 a. 2 ad 1um)*

At the end
of all our suffering,
the thirst still burns –
to know Your face.
Unknown,
You offer Yourself
to our questions;
unknown,
to our hearing.
Daily labour,
sleepless search,
the talk of truth,
woven on ways
of time, and place,
and memory,
the waves of life's great sea,
all comes to rest
on the shore
of the Ultimate.
Your silence is there,
beyond
each speaking.
You embrace
our seeking thought,

when at last
it trusts.
You welcome
our cry
hurled towards Silence.
In You I fall silent:
in Your Word
my words
speak no more.

In You,
most lively quiet,
my questions melt.
Unknown One,
I know You now,
and, my God,
by You
am known!

Thomas reaches the Castle of Maenza, north of Terracina, home of his niece Francesca, wife of Annibaldo, count of Ceccano. While there, he falls ill and hardly eats at all. To encourage him to take some nourishment, his doctor, John di Guido from Piperno, enquires what dish he would especially like. Thomas asks for some fresh herrings, recalling those he enjoyed once in France.[10]

Miraculously, the herrings are found.[11]

Thomas manages to celebrate Mass, and does so with extraordinary intensity, shedding many tears.

[10] Cf. William of Tocco, chap. 56, 129 f.
[11] 'De quibus etiam arengis comedit dictus frater Thomas,' Processus, no. 50, 333.

Once more
this love of earth,
of things savoured,
seen, touched,
things heard and smelt,
of smiles, affection.
Wanting to be faithful
to the Eternal
does not take me
from this humble,
faithful tenderness
for the passing world.
Nothing disappears
from the heart on fire:
all returns
in a last,
most vivid flame.
And all tastes of tears,
of homesickness,
of hope.
It is like a sweat of blood,
which covers all:
what passes
shines bright
in the crucified beauty
of What remains.
All things pass.
All things return.

In that one faithful love
all is suffused
with the one bright light
that remains...

In his niece's home, Thomas relives the memory of his beloved family.[12]

He thinks above all of his brother Rinaldo, a soldier, and a poet of the Sicilian school praised by Dante in his De Vulgari Eloquentia (I, 12). Rinaldo had been valet to Emperor Frederic II, but in 1246 the Emperor had him executed on suspicion of going over to Charles of Anjou, the Pope's ally. In consequence, his family considered him a martyr for the Church's cause. Thomas, who loved him much, had asked the Lord in prayer to reveal to him what had become of Rinaldo, and had received the assurance that his brother's name was written in the book of life.[13]

[12] Thomas's eldest brother, Aimone, who had fallen prisoner during an expedition to the Holy Land and been ransomed upon the intervention of Gregory IX in 1233, remained faithful to the Pope's party for the whole of his life. Of his five sisters, Marotta, the eldest, became abbess of the Convent of St. Mary in Capua and died towards 1259; Theodora married Ruggero, count of San Severino, from whom she had a son, Thomas, who became a Dominican like his uncle; Maria married William of San Severino and they had a daughter, Catherine of Morra, who would supply William of Tocco with many details about the family; Adelasia married Ruggero of Aquila, of whose will Thomas was executor in 1272; Thomas's fifth sister – whose name is unknown – died in infancy, struck by lightning.

[13] 'Frater Thomas petiit a Deo in oratione devota quod... Deus revelaret sibi quid esset de anima domini Raynaldi, fratris sui, quem imperator Fredericus occiderat et ut credebat iniuste; et ipse responsum habuit quod... nomen domini Raynaldi scriptum erat in libro vitae,' Processus, no. 78, 374-376.

47

For others
silence means
heart's emptiness.
For us, though,
silence
is the net of memories,
code of familiar joys,
appointment with shared sorrow,
the word unspoken
speaking the journey shared.
And now that times passed
draw deeper furrows
in our life's wide field;
now that to us –
who set out
all but as one –
more bright appears
to heart's gaze
that final shore,
to have You as my brother
is a strength that enlivens
the journey of my days.
Together, we look forward
with the self-same hope,
we love the same sweet things,
we are welcomed, pilgrims,
by the same Silence,
of which our silence

is footprint
and glimpse.
That You be
is His way
of telling me
He is...[14]

[14] Written for my brother Fabrizio on the occasion of his fiftieth birthday. Here I imagine him – in memory's time beyond time – as Thomas thought of his much beloved brother Rinaldo.

Thomas's life had had its tense and difficult times. Evidence of this is the story that there was an attempt to poison him, ordered by Charles of Anjou and carried out by the doctor sent to examine him at Maenza. This story, though, appears to have been a calumny put about by the enemies of the Anjou family. Before leaving for Lyons, Charles had asked Thomas, 'If the Pope asks you about me, what will you tell him?' only to receive the disquieting reply, 'I will tell him the truth.' Dante gives credence to the story: 'Charles came to Italy; to make amends / he made of Conradin his victim; then, / send Thomas off to Heaven, to make amends' (Purgatorio XX, 67-69: tr. by M. Musa, Bloomington 1981, 216). In any case, the story attests to Thomas's courage; he was a man ever ready to bear witness to the truth.

At the frontier
between abyss and abyss
the soul stands,
pierced by light,
drawn upwards yet,
drawn from below,
on every flank:
it is time now
for the timeless choice.
Who will accept
that death be life
and self-abandonment
the retreat
that saves?
Who – in silence –
will say the word,
intending not
to breach
the Other's mystery?
Unfathomable
this final choice,
Truth which possesses
yet bears not
to be possessed.
Unfathomable
the love
loving without reason,
nor caring

for love's return:
love itself
is all the lover's reason.
The choice now –
flaming arrow
shot across the gulf:
to rush to God
or hesitate an instant,
one last resistance
or abandoned self-abandoning.
For the humble,
the hour of truth,
when all is accomplished.

After spending a few days at the Castle of Maenza, Brother Thomas asks to be taken to the Cistercian abbey of Fossanova: 'If the Lord comes to visit me, it is better he find me in a religious house than in a castle.'[15] Here 'he lay ill for almost a month,' lovingly cared for by the monks, for whom – it is reported – he dictated a short commentary on the Song of Songs. Even though this is very unlikely,[16] it speaks of what must have been, in Thomas's last days, his colloquy of faith and love with his Lord.

[15] 'Si Dominus voluerit me visitare, melius est quod reperiar in domo religiosorum quam in domibus saecularium,' Processus, no. 8, 276 f.

[16] Reported by William of Tocco (chap. 57, 130 f.), but not mentioned by any of the Cistercian witnesses at the process in Naples.

LOVE'S FRIEND IS PAIN

> *'I slept, but my heart kept vigil.*
> *I heard the knock of my beloved.*
> *Open to me...'*
> (Song of Songs 5, 2)

Love's friend
is pain:
longing for the Other,
missing the Absent One,
inexplicable silence
of Him
who all the same
had promised Himself...
Why this interplay
of nights and days,
of words
and stubborn dumbness?
Why be slow to meet,
if this alone dissolves
the pain-filled darkness
of distance?

Your heart
keeps vigil in the night,
keeps vigil
where love's fire grows clear.
Forgetful of self,
you become pure waiting.

Freedom, tested,
sets the table
of encounter.
Only night's beggar
will hear
the voice of the Awaited:
Arise!
Come!

After making his confession to Reginald on 4 or 5 March, Thomas receives Holy Communion and says these words: 'I receive You, the price of my soul's redemption, I receive you, viaticum of my pilgrimage. For love of You I studied, kept vigil, laboured, preached and taught; never have I said a word against You, and if I ever did, it was out of ignorance, and I have not persevered in my error; and if I ever taught anything wrong, I entrust everything to the correction of the Roman Church.'[17]

---

[17] 'Sumo te pretium redemptionis animae meae, sumo te viaticum peregrinationis meae, pro cuius amore studui, vigilavi et laboravi et praedicavi et docui; nihil umquam contra te dixi, sed si quid dixi ignorans, nec sum pertinax in sensu meo; sed si quid male dixi, totum relinquo correctioni Ecclesiae Romanae,' *Processus*, no. 80, 379.

For me
you were
life, food, journey.
For You I lived,
of You I spoke,
in You I was silent.
And now that the last words
fall mute in the great silence
of the time which does not pass,
You are my silence,
You the eternal word
which does not die.
The straw turns to ashes,
but there still burns
the living flame
of Your love:
You remain.
In You I rest,
seed hidden
in the earth.
Dying in You,
I live,
You my inheritance and my crown,
last harbour
of my humble heart.
In You,
no longer being,
I am.

*B*rother Thomas is given the anointing of the sick the following day. He is fully conscious. At first light on Wednesday 7 March he receives the Body of the Lord once more:[18] all is now accomplished. 'The aforementioned doctor died in the year of Our Lord 1274, fourth in the reign of Pope Gregory X, forty-ninth of his life, during the second [imperial] indiction, on the morning of the seventh day of March.'[19]

[18] Processus, no. 49, 332.
[19] 'Obiit autem praedictus Doctor anno Domini millesimo ducentesimo septuagesimo quarto, Pape Gregorii X anno quarto, anno vero vitae suae XLIX, indictione secunda, septimo die Martii, hora matutinali,' William of Tocco, chap. 65, 138.

All is accomplished now:
here in this last silence
beyond being
beyond truth
beyond good,
beyond all beauty,
beyond all my thirsty mind
imagined of You,
beyond the divine,
now, at last
You are
God, not god,
Eternal, not eternal,
Light, not light,
beyond darkness,
beyond the furthest frontier,
ultimate God
You
are.
For You there burns
the straw I was:
in You,
forgetting all,
I find all –
in the greatest of loves,
ocean of the Three,
who are
One.

To You
the cry of the word
that no longer cries.

To you the praise
of silence.

The silence
that is me...

A letter
from Mario Luzi*

Dear Bruno,

Forgive this long delay. I wanted to read your work in the most suitable way, that is in peace, in the calm that is possible here at Pienza, where I am at last. And so now, finally, I have read what you have written. I have to tell you that I regret postponing till today the pleasure and encouragement of reading a text like yours – vivid, full of feeling both received and given, with its simple yet challenging insights.

As we reach the end of this century, with its desperate and arrogant adventure into the senseless and the ambiguous, your work has helped me to think that there is, after all, good to be found in that adventure, in our being anchored to this strong and precious life, which, seen deep down, reveals all its true value. This is a real merit of your text, which touches on more than one aspect of the human condition.

If I limit myself only to the literary aspect of what you have written, I would want to say that it weaves style and rhythm together with wisdom and devotion. Seamlessly, without gaps. And to me this seems no small success....

Pienza, August 1996

* *Mario Luzi (born in 1914) is a key figure in modern Italian poetry.*

Afterword
by Sergio Givone*

Is it possible to let silence speak through words? Is it possible to interpret the mystery of soundlessness in language? Is it possible to unveil the enigma that resists all questioning and yet keep the mystery safe?

Yes, replies Bruno Forte, it is possible, or, rather, it *is not possible except* through poetry. And this is because the words of poetry are a discourse at the very edge of silence, so that, speaking of things, poetry evokes the silence from which they come and from which they receive their meaning. Thus poetry expresses the silence of being, in contrast to discursive words that appear more effective the less they concede to the ambiguity of the inexpressible.

In this way poetry can become the echo of an intense mystical experience, like that of Thomas Aquinas in the last year of his life. Bruno Forte refers especially to the witness of William of Tocco, whose testimony itself seems illuminated 'from above' by a revelation belonging both to religion and to poetry. William tells how Thomas was repeatedly moved – 'as if taken up by the depth of the holy mysteries' – whenever he heard the psalm at Vespers: 'Do not cast me off in the time of old age; do not forsake me when my strength is spent.' And so why not prolong this religious experience by staying on in the dimension most congenial to it? Why not dispose

---

* *Sergio Givone (born in 1944) lectures in Aesthetics at the University of Florence.*

oneself to listen to that which both withdraws from words and yet finds in words a way to reach the human heart? Why not dare the most difficult poetry of all?

Bruno Forte takes this risky and yet necessary step. And he does this entirely aware of what he is about. He begins from the texts which record Thomas's ecstasies. Record? That is certainly not quite the right word. It is more a matter of footprints in which we are allowed to perceive the sign of something more than human – something that overwhelms the one who opens up to and suffers the immense power of the transcendent. Imagine, then, the effect on those who only glimpse the reflection. And yet these signs, these stuttering reports of the disciples point to the very centre of the light and encourage a journey upwards towards it. A journey only possible with poetry's help.

'In the midst of life / I weep for this earth / I love / ... / I weep / because these hands / will no more touch / this matter / fragile yet sublime, / solid yet corruptible, / noble yet suspended / over the abyss of nothingness. / I weep / because these ears / will no more listen / to the music, / tragic yet sweet'. Who is the poet that speaks these words? Is it Thomas, or is it the one who walks humbly with him on his journey towards God, and records what happened? It matters not. In the measure that the poetic word is able to penetrate that experience, so as to translate it into language, a movement of tran-scendence suffuses and animates it, and in fact the subject, the one who uses the first person singular ('I weep') is certainly the writer and so *not* Thomas (who wrote nothing of his experience), but nonetheless it *is*

Thomas. This can be said without any reservation except that it may be drawn up into a higher 'anamnesis', into the making present now of One who the self recognizes as Other, the You in which the self finds a welcome and is 'divinized': 'And You, / do You not weep / with me / in Your eternal / Gethsemane?'

True enough, Thomas writes no longer. Indeed (as Bruno Forte himself recalls, referring to the official minutes of the process of beatification) 'he hung up his writing implements', just as the Hebrew exiles had hung their harps on the willows, unable to sing the Lord's song in a foreign land (Cf. Psalm 137). But precisely then, as the poet says, 'Because of Your flesh / the dead will speak / words full of love'. That this miracle be accomplished, it is not enough to be silent, but to die, and death here is not only our death, but the death of God, in which is included 'the infinite pain of time'. And so, how can we not ask: 'Will words ever be able / to sing / this soul's open wound?' To those who encourage Thomas to take up his work again, since it is too precious to be interrupted (has it not enlightened the world?), he replies: 'I cannot'.

And indeed how could he, if all that he has so far written is, in comparison with what he has seen, no more than straw – something inessential, if not fictitious, at the very least inadequate. And yet everything *must* become straw. It is precisely through this being consumed in the flame of vision that language can hope to 'call forth the abyss', to be the 'merest signpost / to the hidden spring / of speech'. But to repeat the point: what if not poetry, which always and in every case says *two things at once*, can manage effectively to enter into the tragedy of this twoness, in which the unsayable is said on the basis of its negation, of that infinite point in which it disappears?

Hence the difficulty, indeed the impossibility: 'I cannot pass again / the threshold'. Indeed. How can he return to words after entering into silence? 'Words full of love / are what I long / to say to You! But they too – / would they not be / mere straw, / good only to be burnt?' Yet, the poet can ask with Thomas whether, in the midst of this distress, there may still not be found 'the deep secret / of the hidden / pearl?' After all, it is not a matter of a confused swinging between speech and silence, with no central focus. There is a centre, as we have seen: it is the epiphany of the divine, the Eternal. Hence the same movement of appearing and disappearing is present in the sign of a 'clear, sovereign star.'

But does this mean that the star, God's all-encompassing gaze on past, present and future, has necessary consequences? Or does the necessity of being completely transparent to oneself not only not destroy but actually demand freedom? How he forgot the step beyond discursive words was explained by Thomas: the plane of vision, to which all is open and which rests entire in the truth, and the plane of human activity are separate. Seeing does not compel action ... at least as far as philosophy is concerned. But perhaps poetry is more revealing: 'Watched by eternity, / the fleeting moment / tastes / the bitter sweet / fruit of freedom'.

So many questions. No question is ultimate, nor definitive. In the end there is silence. Which, paradox of paradoxes, goes beyond itself. If, on the borders of the latency and the presence of God, questions 'melt', it is the result of the silence of Someone who is thus beyond the dissolution of words, of every word. Our invocation does not plunge into the void of meaninglessness, but into the divine void, into the unfathomable abyss. It is welcomed by God in his mysterious silence, who guards it and keeps it safe. And so it is that silence is not only beyond being, beyond the true and the good, but beyond its very self. 'To you the praise / of silence'. And further yet: May you, Silence, be praised.